GAO

Report to the Committee on Armed Services, U.S. Senate

I0426060

September 2012

MILITARY DEPENDENT STUDENTS

Better Oversight Needed to Improve Services for Children with Special Needs

G A O

Accountability ★ Integrity ★ Reliability

MILITARY DEPENDENT STUDENTS

Better Oversight Needed to Improve Services for Children with Special Needs

G A O
Accountability * Integrity * Reliability

Highlights

Highlights of GAO-12-680, a report to the Committee on Armed Services, U.S. Senate

Why GAO Did This Study

DOD operates a worldwide school system to meet the educational needs of military dependents. Questions have arisen about whether DOD is meeting the special needs of some of these children, such as those with learning disabilities. In response to a mandate in the National Defense Authorization Act for Fiscal Year 2011, GAO reviewed (1) how DOD provides special education services; (2) how DOD entities coordinate to assign families overseas and how schools might be affected; (3) what challenges, if any, families face in accessing DOD services for their children with special educational needs and obtaining related information; and (4) what steps, if any, DOD is taking to enhance screening and overseas assignment for families with children with special educational needs. GAO reviewed relevant federal laws and regulations, analyzed DOD documents and data, and conducted interviews with officials from multiple DOD entities, including schools. GAO also held 22 focus groups with parents of children with special needs during site visits and phone interviews at eight military installations worldwide.

What GAO Recommends

GAO recommends that the Secretary of Defense (1) ensure the military branches medically and educationally screen all school-age children before relocation overseas; (2) direct OSN to establish benchmarks and performance goals for the EFM program; and (3) direct OSN to develop and implement a process for ensuring the branches' compliance with EFM program requirements. DOD generally agreed with the recommendations.

View GAO-12-680. For more information, contact George Scott at (202) 512-7215 or scottg@gao.gov.

What GAO Found

The Department of Defense (DOD) provides special education services through a complex system that varies by location. Domestically, DOD provides special education mainly within DOD schools. In contrast, DOD schools overseas vary in the types and levels of disabilities they are readily equipped to serve. For example, DOD schools in Ramstein, Germany, are equipped to serve children with severe disabilities of any type, whereas schools in some other overseas installations have no pre-established special education programs of any kind.

Overseas assignment of servicemembers with children with special educational needs requires coordination between the military branches through their Exceptional Family Member (EFM) programs and the DOD Education Activity—the office that oversees education of military dependent children in DOD schools. Each branch implements its own processes for screening military families and assigning servicemembers to locations where there are school services that can meet their families' needs. However, impediments to effective placements may strain school resources. More specifically, ineffective screenings may result in families being placed in locations where schools are not readily equipped to serve certain needs. For example, we found one case in which a school that only had programs in place for students with mild disabilities received a student with severe needs who had not been educationally screened.

Families in many of GAO's focus groups were generally satisfied with the services DOD provided their children with special needs once they received them, but they felt that the limited availability of special education and medical specialists overseas presented challenges. Some parents were concerned their children were not receiving all the services they needed, partly due to difficulties DOD schools encounter hiring and retaining special education staff, especially overseas. While the military branches provide family support services, parents in our focus groups also indicated they lacked information about obtaining special education and related medical services. DOD is taking some steps to provide better information to families, but the extent to which these efforts are helping them is unclear.

DOD's recently established Office of Special Needs (OSN) is responsible for enhancing and monitoring support for military families with special needs. OSN and the military branches have initiated efforts to improve screening and overseas assignment of military families with special needs. However, it is unclear when some of these efforts will be completed. Moreover, while OSN was established in part to enhance and monitor the military branches' support for families with special needs, it has limited enforcement authority and oversight over the branches' EFM programs. Specifically, it is limited in the extent to which it can compel the branches to comply with DOD or service-level program requirements, and it has no direct means by which to hold them accountable if they fail to do so. In addition, DOD currently lacks agencywide benchmarks and performance goals for all components of the EFM program. As a result, it cannot assess the effectiveness of the branches' EFM programs and ensure that improvements are made when needed. Without overall performance information to proactively identify emerging problem areas, some of the branches have had to conduct investigations to address problems after they have arisen.

_____ United States Government Accountability Office

Contents

Figures

Abbreviations

DOD	Department of Defense
DODEA	Department of Defense Education Activity
EDIS	Educational and Developmental Intervention Services
EFM (Program)	Exceptional Family Member Program
IDEA	Individuals with Disabilities Education Act
IEP	Individualized Education Program
NDAA	National Defense Authorization Act
OSN	Office of Special Needs

G A O
Accountability * Integrity * Reliability

United States Government Accountability Office
Washington, DC 20548

September 10, 2012

The Honorable Carl Levin
Chairman
The Honorable John S. McCain
Ranking Member
Committee on Armed Services
United States Senate

Military families who have children with special needs, such as communication impairments or learning disabilities, face a unique set of challenges, in part due to their frequent moves within the United States and to overseas installations.[1] Recent executive branch, congressional, and advocacy group initiatives have focused on increasing support for these families. For example, in 2011 the White House issued a report making the care and support of military families a top national security policy priority, including ensuring excellence in military children's education and development.

About 12 percent of the approximately 85,000 children enrolled in Department of Defense (DOD) schools worldwide received special education services in the 2011-12 school year, and over half of these students were in schools overseas.[2] DOD is required to provide special education and related services for children with disabilities who attend DOD schools, as prescribed in the Individuals with Disabilities Education Act (IDEA).[3]

Given the important role DOD schools play in serving highly mobile military families, questions have arisen regarding whether DOD is meeting the complex needs of students with special needs.[4] In response

---

[1]For the purpose of this report, the terms "special needs" and "disabilities" will be used interchangeably, unless indicated otherwise.

[2]Data are as of January 2012.

[3]Codified at 20 U.S.C. §§ 1400 to 1482.

[4]The term "special needs" encompasses both children with disabilities that receive special education services as well as children that meet the definition of special needs under the military branches' Exceptional Family Member programs, both of which are discussed later in this report.

to a mandate in the Senate report accompanying the National Defense Authorization Act (NDAA) for Fiscal Year 2011,[5] GAO examined (1) how DOD provides special education services; (2) how DOD entities coordinate to assign servicemembers accompanied by their families to overseas locations and how schools might be affected; (3) what challenges, if any, families face in accessing DOD services for their children with special educational needs and obtaining related information; and (4) what steps, if any, DOD is taking to enhance assignment coordination for servicemembers who have children with special educational needs.

To address these questions, we reviewed relevant federal laws and regulations and analyzed DOD policy and guidance documents. We also obtained data from the DOD Education Activity (DODEA)—the office that oversees the education of military dependent children in DOD schools—on the number and characteristics of students in DOD schools receiving special education services in the United States and overseas, as well as quantitative and qualitative data on educational screenings and family assignment concerns. We determined these data to be reliable for the purpose of describing the population of children with disabilities in DOD schools and reporting information about screenings and assignment concerns. We conducted site visits to five military installations in Europe and two in the United States, as well as telephone interviews with agency officials at one military installation in the Pacific. We selected these locations based on several criteria, including the number of children with disabilities enrolled in DOD schools, the level of special education services schools were equipped to provide, variation in urban and remote areas, and variation among the four military branches. During our site visits and Pacific teleconference, we conducted meetings with officials from 15 schools and held 22 focus groups with the parents of students receiving special education services to discuss their perceptions of the services their children have received. While the results of these focus groups cannot be generalized to all parents of children with disabilities, nor are they representative of the population of parents, common responses across groups and recurring themes provide some degree of validation. We also interviewed DODEA officials in the United States and overseas, including district and school officials, such as principals, special education coordinators, and teachers. In addition, we interviewed officials

---

[5]S. Rep. No. 111-201, at 138 (2010).

from DOD's Office of Special Needs (OSN), the military branches, subject matter experts, and advocacy groups. Finally, we met with representatives from other DOD entities, including the military branches' Educational and Developmental Intervention Services (EDIS) and the Exceptional Family Member (EFM) programs involved in screening and supporting this population. Appendix I provides a detailed description of our scope and methodology.

We conducted this performance audit from May 2011 through September 2012 in accordance with generally accepted government auditing standards. Those standards require that we plan and perform the audit to obtain sufficient, appropriate evidence to provide a reasonable basis for our findings and conclusions based on our audit objectives. We believe that the evidence obtained provides a reasonable basis for our findings and conclusions based on our audit objectives.

Background

DOD Schools and Students with Disabilities

DOD operates a worldwide school system to meet the educational needs of military dependent students and others, such as the children of DOD's civilian employees overseas. DODEA oversees the management and operation of 196 schools in seven states; Puerto Rico and Guam; and 12 foreign countries. DODEA has organized its schools into three areas—the United States, Europe, and the Pacific—and multiple districts within each area. About 66 percent (130 of 196) of DOD schools are located overseas serving about 68 percent of the student population (approximately 58,000 of 85,000 children) (see fig. 1). The overseas schools are mainly concentrated in Germany and Japan, where the United States built military installations after World War II. Almost all the domestic schools are in the southeastern United States.

Figure 1: Location of DOD Schools and Number of Students Receiving Special Education Services, January 2012

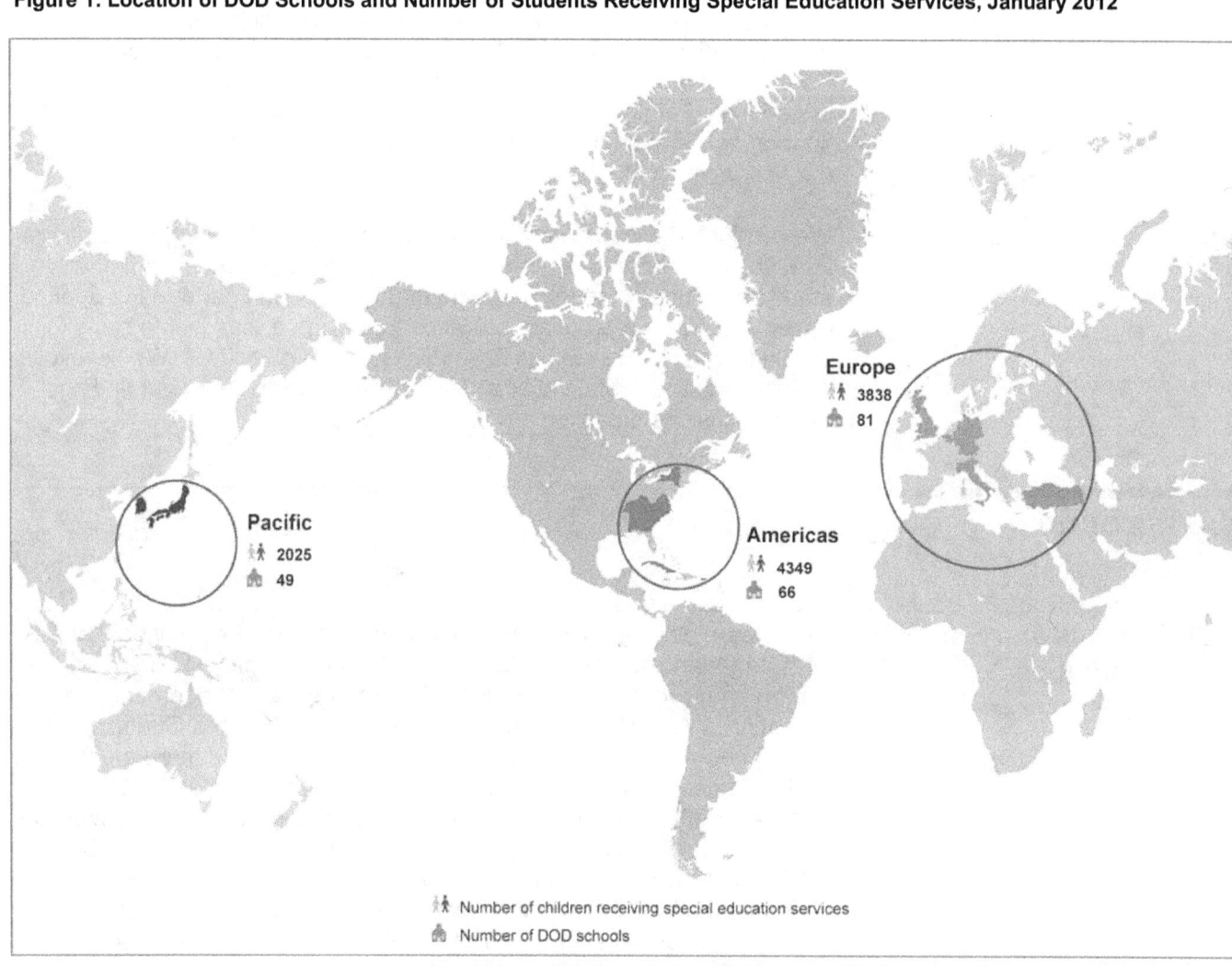

Pacific
👥 2025
⛪ 49

Americas
👥 4349
⛪ 66

Europe
👥 3838
⛪ 81

👥 Number of children receiving special education services
⛪ Number of DOD schools

Source: GAO presentation of general locations of DOD schools, map (Map Resources).

DOD schools provide a comprehensive kindergarten through 12th grade curriculum.[6] Approximately 12 percent (or about 10,200 students) of all students received special education services in the 2011-12 school year.

[6]DOD also provides pre-kindergarten programs for children between the ages of 3 and 5 in its domestic schools. However, the overseas schools only provide pre-kindergarten programs for children with disabilities.

GAO-12-680 Military Dependent Students

As of January 2012, the most prevalent disabilities among children enrolled in DOD schools were communication impairments (such as speech and language impairments), specific learning disabilities, and developmental delays, cumulatively representing about 71 percent of this population (see fig. 2).[7] Appendix II provides DOD's categories and definitions of disabilities. While some children may have more than one type of disability, DODEA bases its criteria for determining eligibility for receiving special education services on the primary type of disability that has the greatest educational impact.

---

[7]The total number of children used as the basis for these calculations is about 9,200, rather than the 10,200 reported above. This is primarily because, at any given point in time, some children's special education eligibility is under review, and DODEA's database does not capture their disability type.

Figure 2: Primary Type of Disability of Children Enrolled in DOD Schools, January 2012

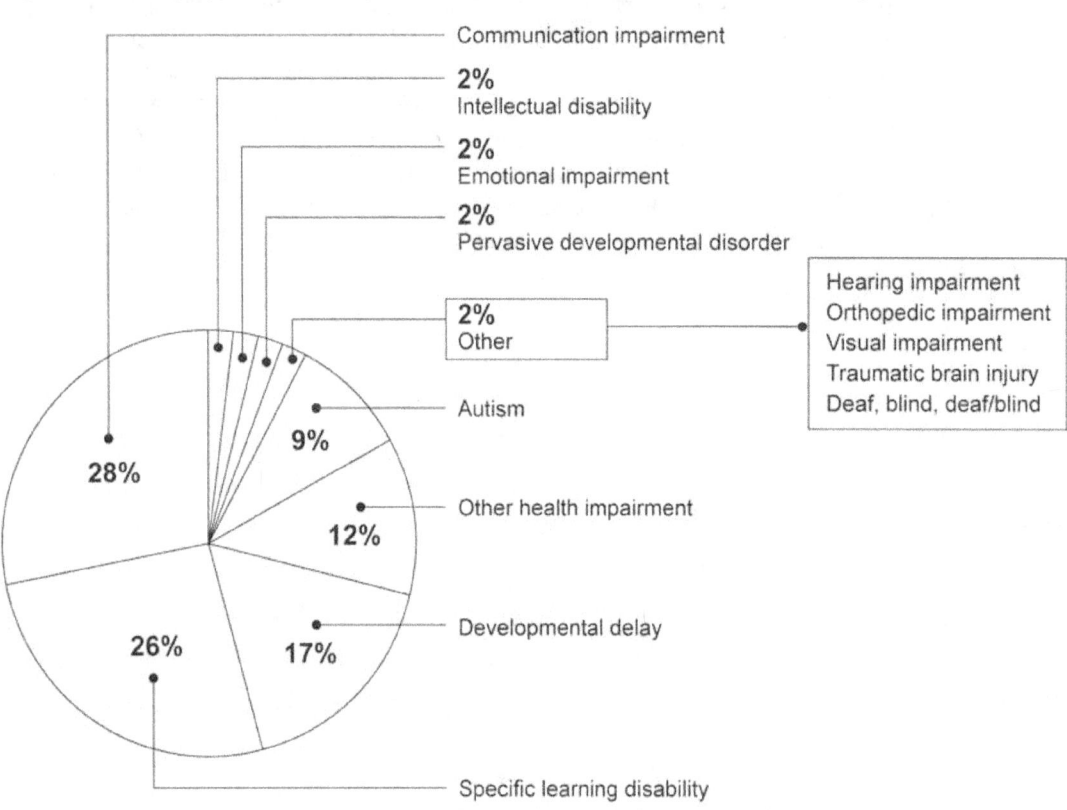

Source: GAO presentation of Department of Defense Education Activity data.

Although DOD schools do not receive IDEA funding, DOD is required to provide in its educational programs the substantive rights, protections, and procedural safeguards for students with disabilities under IDEA.[8] Specifically, DOD is required to provide these children early intervention services, and special education and related services. For children ages 3 to 21, this includes identifying and evaluating eligible children; developing and implementing an individualized education program (IEP) for such students (see fig. 3); and providing the students special education and

---

[8] 10 U.S.C. § 2164(f), 20 U.S.C. § 927(c).

related services.[9] The military medical departments—through their EDIS programs—are responsible for providing selected related services as well as completing evaluations for certain disabilities, such as autism or visual or hearing impairments, that may require medical expertise.

---

[9]DOD Instruction 1342.12, *Provision of Early Intervention and Special Education Services to Eligible DoD Dependents*, April 11, 2005. Special education is specially designed instruction which is provided at no cost to parents to meet the unique needs of a child with a disability. Related services include speech-language pathology and audiology, psychological services, physical and occupational therapy, early identification and assessment of disabilities in children, and other services. In this report we refer to special education and related services as special education services.

Figure 3: IEP Process for DOD Schools

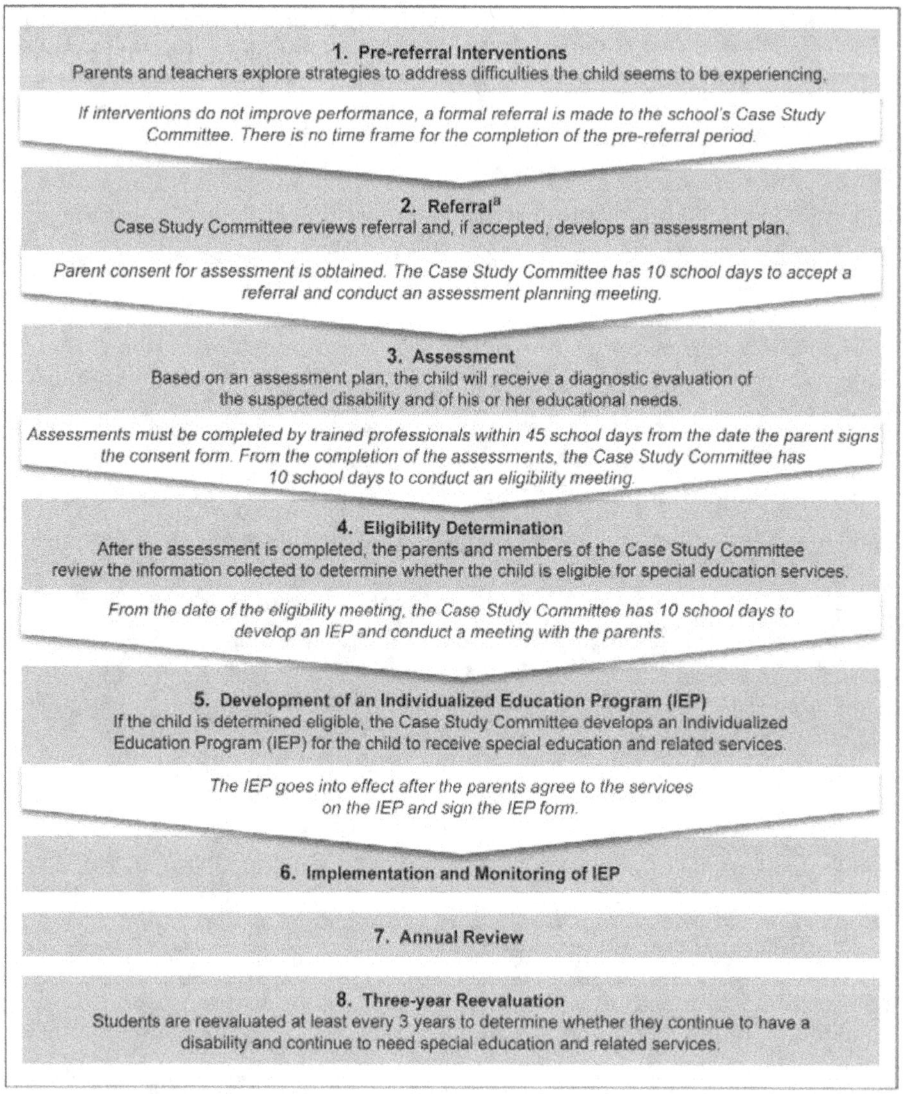

| 1. Pre-referral Interventions |
| Parents and teachers explore strategies to address difficulties the child seems to be experiencing. |

If interventions do not improve performance, a formal referral is made to the school's Case Study Committee. There is no time frame for the completion of the pre-referral period.

| 2. Referral[a] |
| Case Study Committee reviews referral and, if accepted, develops an assessment plan. |

Parent consent for assessment is obtained. The Case Study Committee has 10 school days to accept a referral and conduct an assessment planning meeting.

| 3. Assessment |
| Based on an assessment plan, the child will receive a diagnostic evaluation of the suspected disability and of his or her educational needs. |

Assessments must be completed by trained professionals within 45 school days from the date the parent signs the consent form. From the completion of the assessments, the Case Study Committee has 10 school days to conduct an eligibility meeting.

| 4. Eligibility Determination |
| After the assessment is completed, the parents and members of the Case Study Committee review the information collected to determine whether the child is eligible for special education services. |

From the date of the eligibility meeting, the Case Study Committee has 10 school days to develop an IEP and conduct a meeting with the parents.

| 5. Development of an Individualized Education Program (IEP) |
| If the child is determined eligible, the Case Study Committee develops an Individualized Education Program (IEP) for the child to receive special education and related services. |

The IEP goes into effect after the parents agree to the services on the IEP and sign the IEP form.

| 6. Implementation and Monitoring of IEP |

| 7. Annual Review |

| 8. Three-year Reevaluation |
| Students are reevaluated at least every 3 years to determine whether they continue to have a disability and continue to need special education and related services. |

Source: GAO analysis of DOD documents.

[a]The Case Study Committee is a multidisciplinary team of special educators, regular educators, related services personnel, administrators, and parents, where appropriate.

Exceptional Family Member Program

To implement DOD's policy regarding overseas travel for eligible military dependents with special needs, each branch is required to establish its own EFM program for active duty servicemembers.[10] The Army set up the first EFM program in 1979; since that time, the Air Force, Marine Corps, and Navy have also established EFM programs. EFM programs have three components—identification and enrollment, assignment coordination, and family support services.

- **Identification and Enrollment.** Active duty servicemembers with eligible family members are required to enroll in the EFM program for their branch to document dependents' special needs, so that medical and educational personnel can review the availability of medical and educational resources in planned assignment locations.[11]

- **Assignment Coordination.** Each military branch is required to identify, document, and consider a military family member's special needs during the process of assigning servicemembers to a particular installation. Screening and assignment coordination occur when the branch's personnel command requests that medical and/or educational professionals review a family member's documented needs to determine the availability of DOD's specialized medical and educational services at a planned location.

- **Family Support.** Each military branch's EFM program is required to include a family support component. EFM program family support personnel assist families with special needs by helping them identify and access programs and services. Services may include information and referrals for military and community services, education and training about issues related to the special needs, local school

---

[10]Department of Defense Instruction 1315.19, *Authorizing Special Needs Family Members Travel Overseas at Government Expense (*Dec. 20, 2005). DOD officials stated that while this guidance was intended for overseas travel, DOD also uses it to identify family members with special medical needs within the United States.

[11]An eligible family member is generally defined as (1) a spouse, child, or dependent adult who, regardless of age, has special medical needs and requires medical services for a chronic condition such as asthma, attention deficit disorder, diabetes, multiple sclerosis, etc.; receives ongoing services from a medical specialist; or has significant behavioral health concerns; or (2) a child (birth through 21 years) with special educational needs who is eligible for, or receives, special education services through an IEP; or Early Intervention Services through an Individualized Family Service Plan. Civilian families are not eligible for EFM programs.

information, nonclinical case management, and assistance transitioning between installations.

The NDAA for Fiscal Year 2010 expanded support for military families with special needs.[12] While initial EFM program requirements only included identification and enrollment and assignment coordination, the Act requires DOD to develop and implement a comprehensive policy on family support. While the Army and Marine Corps incorporated family support programs into their EFM programs prior to this requirement, the Air Force and Navy began incorporating family support programs in 2010. The Act also created the Office of Community Support for Military Families with Special Needs, referred to as OSN, and specified its responsibilities to include

- developing and implementing a comprehensive policy for the support of military families with special needs,

- establishing and overseeing associated programs,

- identifying gaps in DOD services for military families with special needs,

- developing plans to address gaps in DOD services through appropriate mechanisms such as enhancing resources and training, and ensuring the provision of special assistance,

- monitoring the programs of the military departments for the assignment of servicemembers who are members of families with special needs and the programs in support of such families, and

- advising the Secretary of Defense on the adequacy of such programs in conjunction with DOD budgeting and planning activities.

---

[12]National Defense Authorization Act for Fiscal Year 2010, Pub. L. No. 111-84, § 563, 123 Stat. 2190, 2304 (2009).

GAO-12-680 Military Dependent Students

DOD Provides Special Education Services through a Complex System That Varies by Location

Like public schools in the United States, DOD is required to provide special education and related services necessary to meet the unique needs of eligible students. As needed, DOD schools provide special education services in all schools worldwide and related services (such as occupational and physical therapy) in its domestic schools only. Overseas, each branch's medical department provides related services to eligible students through its EDIS program. A child with a disability may receive services from some or all of the DOD entities shown in figure 4, depending on the family's location.

Figure 4: DOD Entities That Provide Special Education Services

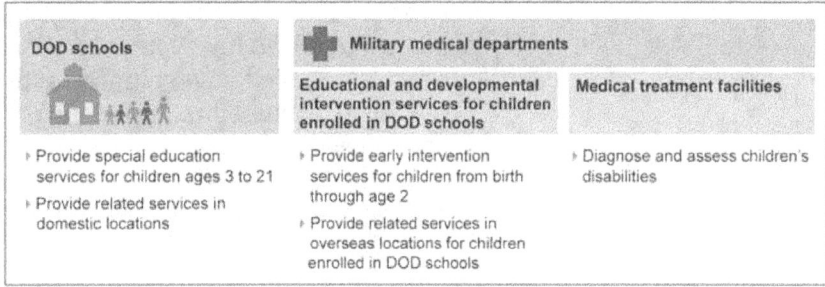

Source: GAO analysis of DOD documents.

Services for children with disabilities in DOD schools may include consultation by special educators to general classroom teachers or instruction in a special education classroom for part or all of the school day. In addition to special and general education teachers, DOD schools employ paraprofessionals—who assist and support teachers— and specialists, such as speech and language therapists. DOD schools in the United States also provide related services, such as physical and occupational therapy.

The military branches' medical departments provide different types of services for children with disabilities through their EDIS programs. EDIS helps identify children with disabilities and delivers early intervention services to eligible infants and toddlers, from birth through age 2. EDIS also provides medical assessments necessary to determine children's eligibility for special education services. For example, in order to provide special education services for children with emotional impairments or autism spectrum disorders, DODEA requires medical evaluations and diagnoses by qualified medical professionals, such as developmental pediatricians, psychologists, or psychiatrists. Although military families may use civilian providers in the United States, when stationed overseas, only military providers may provide these diagnoses for children attending DOD schools. Overseas, EDIS also provides related services for children enrolled in DOD schools.

Domestic DOD schools provide special education for all types and levels of disabilities, mainly within DOD schools. However, according to DOD, in certain cases students may receive services from external service providers that DOD contracts with or they may be placed in local public schools. Overseas, the military branches and DODEA have implemented a system of specific, pre-established programs for different types of disabilities and levels of services in each school. For example, schools in Ramstein, Germany, have programs designed to serve children with all types of disabilities, whereas schools in Iwakuni, Japan, have programs that serve only a few types of disabilities, and the Seville Elementary School in Spain has no programs for any type of disability. Agency officials explained that this variation is a function of the size of the military community and the needs of the military. To help facilitate intra-agency communication about these differences, DOD developed a directory that indicates which pre-established programs are available in each school overseas. (See figure 5 for an excerpt of this directory.)

Figure 5: Examples of Variation in Levels of Services Available at DOD Schools Overseas

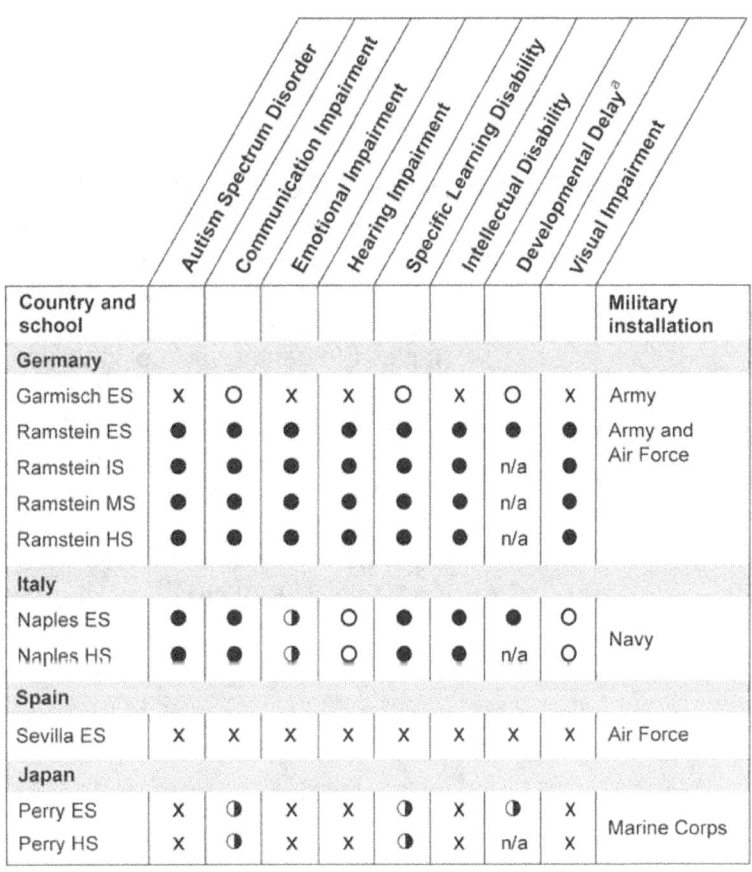

Country and school	Autism Spectrum Disorder	Communication Impairment	Emotional Impairment	Hearing Impairment	Specific Learning Disability	Intellectual Disability	Developmental Delay[a]	Visual Impairment	Military installation
Germany									
Garmisch ES	X	O	X	X	O	X	O	X	Army
Ramstein ES	●	●	●	●	●	●	●	●	Army and Air Force
Ramstein IS	●	●	●	●	●	●	n/a	●	
Ramstein MS	●	●	●	●	●	●	n/a	●	
Ramstein HS	●	●	●	●	●	●	n/a	●	
Italy									
Naples ES	●	●	◑	O	●	●	●	O	Navy
Naples HS	●	●	◑	O	●	●	n/a	O	
Spain									
Sevilla ES	X	X	X	X	X	X	X	X	Air Force
Japan									
Perry ES	X	◑	X	X	◑	X	◑	X	Marine Corps
Perry HS	X	◑	X	X	◑	X	n/a	X	

X   No pre-established program

O   Pre-established program for mild disabilities[b]

◑   Pre-established program for moderate disabilities[c]

●   Pre-established program for severe disabilities[d]

Source: Department of Defense Directory, DoD Dependents Schools (DoDDS) and Educational and Developmental Intervention Services (EDIS) (including Cuba, Guam, and Puerto Rico), Early Intervention, Special Education and Related Services in OCONUS Communities.

Notes: All disabilities reflect a continuum of severity, ranging from mild to moderate to severe. The types of services provided and the levels of disabilities are described in detail in the DOD Services Directory for overseas locations. Below are some examples of the types of services provided for each level. However, the descriptions are neither complete nor representative of all disability types.

[a]Developmental delay is a disability category for children from birth through age 7. Therefore, the classification of a developmental delay does not apply in intermediate, middle, or high schools.

GAO-12-680 Military Dependent Students

[b]For mild disabilities, children are typically accommodated in the general education classroom setting and receive needed services through school resources or itinerant specialists. There are no schools with pre-established programs for mild Autism Spectrum Disorder, Emotional Impairment, or Intellectual Disability.

[c]For most types of moderate disabilities, students receive the majority of their instruction in the general education classroom and may also receive supplemental instruction in a resource room.

[d]For severe disabilities, children may receive instruction in a variety of settings, including the general education classroom and a self-contained environment.

Moreover, DOD schools provide different levels of service for each type of disability, as indicated by the circles in the DOD directory excerpt shown in figure 5. For example, Garmisch Elementary School in Germany has a program to provide services in the general education classroom for children with the mildest forms of specific learning disabilities. In contrast, Naples Elementary School in Italy is equipped to provide individualized instruction in a separate classroom setting for children with the most severe types of specific learning disabilities. Schools in Ramstein, Germany, are equipped to serve children with severe disabilities of any type. Nonetheless, consistent with IDEA requirements, it is DOD policy that all schools must provide special education services to all students with such needs, regardless of the types or severity of students' needs or the school's location.

Military Branches Screen Families and Consult with DODEA to Assign Families to Overseas Locations, but Ineffective Processes May Strain School Resources

Military Branches' Processes to Coordinate Overseas Assignment of Servicemembers with Families with Special Needs Are Not Always Effective

Because DOD schools in overseas communities are designated to serve children with certain types and levels of disabilities, the military branches and DODEA are required to coordinate the overseas assignment of servicemembers with families with special needs, including all children with IEPs.[13] All family members who are seeking a move overseas must be screened by the relevant branch's medical department for medical and educational needs in addition to other factors that might inhibit travel overseas, such as financial problems. If the medical screening identifies an EFM program-enrollable condition, the servicemember is referred for EFM program enrollment.

Each branch implements its EFM program differently, and the branches' screening and assignment coordination processes also vary somewhat. Generally, through a process referred to as EFM program assignment coordination, the servicemember's personnel office coordinates with the medical department to verify the availability of medical services in the planned location overseas. During this process, the military branch is also required to coordinate with DODEA about the educational programs available. DODEA makes a recommendation based on the services available at the schools, and the branch's medical department makes a recommendation about the availability of medical services. The military branch then determines whether the servicemember and his or her family should proceed to the planned location. Depending on the recommendations of both medical and educational reviewers, the servicemember may be approved for travel accompanied by family

---

[13]Sections 5.4.3, E4.1 and E4.2 of Department of Defense Instruction 1315.19.

members, recommended to relocate to a different location, or allowed to take an unaccompanied tour. However, according to DODEA and one branch's military officials, the installation's command personnel may override a recommendation for an unaccompanied tour and allow the servicemember to bring the family if he or she has special skills that are needed at an installation.

Each year, some military families with children with special educational needs are sent to locations that are not prepared to serve their children's needs upon arrival. This may occur either due to a "screening failure" (i.e., when an educational screening did not occur) or an "assignment concern" (i.e., when the family was screened but the child was nonetheless enrolled in a school unequipped to meet his or her needs). DODEA records the number of screenings completed and assignment concerns, as well as the reasons for such concerns. DODEA data show that since school year 2008-09, there have been 93 instances when children were educationally screened, but still arrived at a school that did not have programs in place to meet their needs.[14] This may have occurred because (1) the student's needs were more severe than the educational or medical screening indicated, (2) the military overrode DODEA's assignment recommendation, or (3) the servicemember was approved for one location but was reassigned to another. Moreover, several DODEA and school officials we interviewed confirmed that a number of children with special educational needs who were not screened have enrolled in their schools. For example, school officials in Naples said that a few years ago, the school received 44 incoming students with IEPs, but only four of those students had been educationally screened through the EFM program. According to OSN officials, schools are generally able to accommodate children with mild disabilities regardless of the location, and such cases would not be recorded as assignment concerns. However, DODEA officials overseas also stated that when children with severe disabilities are sent to locations that do not have appropriate pre-existing programs, even a very small number of these cases can require substantial additional resources. According to a Navy EFM program official at an installation we visited,

---

[14]According to a DODEA official, the office does not maintain data on the number of children with special needs who should have been educationally screened. DODEA data show that over 5,000 children were educationally screened during this same time frame. Data reported are as of April 2012.

GAO-12-680 Military Dependent Students

screening and assignment coordination failures could cost the military up to $100,000 per incident.

Underenrollment and Circumvention of EFM Procedures Hinder Program Effectiveness

Although all four branches require EFM program enrollment for eligible servicemembers, underenrollment in and circumvention of EFM programs were cited repeatedly as concerns during our interviews and site visits. Senior OSN officials estimated that about half the families with children with special needs who are eligible to enroll in the EFM program have not done so. They attributed underenrollment to several factors, including that some families having children with very mild disabilities may think they are not eligible for the program or may not be aware it exists. DODEA's Europe area and military officials at three of the eight installations included in our study explained that more families are eligible to enroll in EFM programs than have done so. OSN and military officials at three installations also explained that families with special needs may not realize they are required to enroll in EFM programs. DOD officials also explained that a family might be using an off-base medical provider who is not aware of the program. An EFM program official from one installation added that families who rarely relocate may not understand why it is important to enroll. Another EFM program official from a different installation acknowledged that more work needs to be done to raise awareness and enroll families in EFM programs.

Servicemembers may also intentionally circumvent educational screening and EFM enrollment. More specifically, servicemembers sometimes avoid identifying their children's special educational needs by declining special education services or inaccurately completing relevant forms, according to DODEA officials in Europe and the Pacific, as well as other DOD entities we interviewed. Senior OSN officials believe that a fair number of families intentionally opt not to enroll in the EFM program because some are concerned that enrollment may adversely affect servicemembers' careers. They noted that there is a perceived stigma associated with EFM enrollment among servicemembers. Some servicemembers have also been known to travel with their families against recommendation and once on base, request approval from the installation leadership for the family to stay, according to DODEA and military officials at one installation. In seven of our focus groups, parents said they felt that enrolling in EFM would hurt their chances of being assigned to a position or location they desire. However, DOD policy states that servicemembers with children with special educational needs should be assigned to appropriate locations overseas consistent with the needs of the military and the career of the servicemember. According to senior OSN and military officials at two installations, EFM enrollment does not limit servicemembers' career opportunities. They noted that servicemembers can accept an unaccompanied tour to the desired location or seek a different assignment that would better support the family's needs if the initially planned location is not suitable.

EFM programs may not be as effective as they could be due to inconsistent policy enforcement regarding enrollment. DOD policy provides that a servicemember who fails or refuses to provide the information required for overseas screening and assignment or knowingly provides false information may be subject to disciplinary action and administrative sanctions, including denial of command sponsorship.[15] However, OSN and military officials we spoke to at two installations indicated that installation commanders rarely take such disciplinary actions.

Medical screening failures may also contribute to underenrollment in EFM programs. More specifically, some special educational needs are identified when families complete medical screenings for overseas assignments. However, officials from OSN and a military branch explained that sometimes these needs are not identified during screenings, resulting in families not being enrolled in EFM programs. For example, if a servicemember's child is diagnosed with autism by a civilian provider, the military's overseas screening personnel may not be aware of it—since, according to officials from this branch and DODEA, they only have access to records from military hospitals or treatment facilities— unless families disclose this information. Senior DOD officials stated that they believe such failures are uncommon and have minimal impact on EFM program enrollment.

In addition, some branches' EFM programs face administrative challenges that may contribute to underenrollment of families with special needs. A military official from one installation observed that EFM program staff often do not complete the EFM program paperwork or they take a significant amount of time to do so because other duties take priority. For example, officials from two installations said that ideally enrollment should occur within 4 to 6 weeks, but can sometimes take several months for the process to be completed. Moreover, officials at two installations from one

---

[15]Section E5.2.3 of Department of Defense Instruction 1315.19.

GAO-12-680 Military Dependent Students

military branch told us that enrollment forms were not always forwarded to the receiving installation for review.

Failures to Screen and Coordinate Assignments May Strain School Resources

When screening and assignment processes are ineffective, students may arrive at schools that are not immediately equipped to meet their needs. Officials at some schools we visited told us it can be difficult to accommodate students whose needs they are not structured to serve. DODEA district and area office officials concurred, and noted that this is one of the most significant challenges that schools overseas face. To meet the needs of students, schools may need to reallocate or increase staff and other resources, which can be difficult with limited resources.

According to a senior DODEA official, the local district or area administrative offices will first attempt to shift existing resources to meet the needs of students. Typically, a school might bus a student to another location or hire a paraprofessional. However, if necessary, DODEA will purchase new equipment or hire a teacher, a process that can be lengthy in some instances. For example, during our review of DODEA's screening and assignment concern database, we found one case in which a school overseas that did not have pre-existing programs in place for students with severe cognitive disabilities received such a student. The student's family had not gone through EFM program screening before the servicemember's authorization to travel was approved. Once the child's educational records were reviewed, travel was not recommended for the family, but the family arrived nonetheless. As a result, the school had to expend additional resources to meet the student's needs.

In contrast to military personnel, civilian families are not required to enroll in EFM programs or to undergo medical screenings prior to relocating overseas. According to DOD officials, under federal law[16] human resource offices are prohibited from asking civilian employees whether their family members have certain medical conditions or other special needs and cannot bar employment or relocation to overseas installations based on such factors. However, according to DOD policy, DOD human resource offices are responsible for providing information to civilian employees regarding the educational and medical services available at

---

[16]The Genetic Information Nondiscrimination Act (Pub. L. No. 110-233, 122 Stat. 881) prohibits employers from requesting genetic information, including family medical history, from their employees.

overseas installations, so that the civilian employee or selectee may make an informed choice regarding whether to accept the overseas position. DOD human resource offices are also required to provide a point of contact to answer applicants' questions.

Officials from two schools we visited also said that because civilian families do not undergo any systematic screening before transferring overseas, they tend to have the most severe needs. Senior DOD officials, however, told us they do not maintain data on whether civilian families have more severe needs than active duty families. A school official at an installation in Europe told us that the majority of students with severe special needs enrolled in schools on that installation are civilians, and that military dependents with similar needs would have been identified and likely prevented from transferring there during the screening and assignment process. According to data provided by DOD, as of January 2012, there were approximately 1,100 children with special needs from civilian families enrolled in DODEA schools.

Families Generally Satisfied with Special Education Services, but Face Challenges Obtaining Them

Limited Educational and Medical Specialists in Some Locations Pose Challenges for Families, and Schools Struggle to Hire and Retain Staff

Families in 21 out of the 22 focus groups we held told us they were generally satisfied with the special education services their children received in DOD schools once they received them. Further, participants in 10 focus groups said that special education services in DOD schools were superior to those in the non-DOD schools their children had attended. In fact, one focus group participant in Germany was so pleased with the special education services her children had received at DOD schools that she wanted to remain on the installation for several additional years so her children could graduate from them.

Despite families' general satisfaction with services once their children received them, participants in 16 out of 22 focus groups we held reported facing challenges obtaining these services due to the limited availability of related service providers available on military installations, particularly overseas. More specifically, participants in seven focus groups said they believe that there are shortages of occupational therapists or physical therapists at certain schools. For example, a parent in one focus group believed her child was not receiving necessary services as often as she felt was warranted. In the 2008-09 school year, DODEA issued 285 reports of unavailability of medically related services for military dependents in the Pacific region due to the number of vacancies at Navy EDIS clinics and delays in filling positions.[17] According to these reports, unavailable services included diagnostic evaluations, social work services, as well as occupational and physical therapy. Since 2009, many of these cases have been resolved.[18] In school years 2009-10 and 2011-12, there were 41 reports of unavailability of medically related services.

In addition, participants in six of our focus groups expressed concern with perceived shortages of paraprofessionals to assist special education teachers, and participants in four focus groups also stated that they believed there was high turnover among them. Officials from three schools we spoke with and DODEA officials from one district indicated that there are shortages of paraprofessionals or high turnover among them. The high turnover rate among paraprofessionals can be especially disruptive for children with special needs, who thrive on consistency, according to parents in three of our focus groups.

Participants in seven focus groups told us it has been difficult for them to obtain medical services for their children. Since IEPs require medical diagnoses for some conditions, limited medical services can directly affect students' educational progress. According to DODEA guidelines, certain impairments require medical reports from appropriate specialists, which can include developmental pediatricians, psychologists, autism clinicians, and audiologists, among others. Some school, DODEA, and EFM program officials we met with confirmed that it can be difficult for families to obtain medical services on base. For example, while DOD officials told us that military families have greater access to developmental

---

[17]Reports of unavailability of medically related services are filed when a DOD school determines that children with disabilities have unmet medical needs.

[18]According to DODEA's Annual Compliance Report for 2009, several of the cases were resolved and make-up services were provided to many students in the summer of 2009. In addition, DODEA's Annual Compliance Report for 2010 states that the number of reports on unavailability of medically related services was substantially reduced in the 2009-10 school year as a result of ongoing oversight and corrective actions implemented by the Navy.

pediatricians than civilians, officials at a domestic school we visited said that waiting lists for developmental pediatricians at the military medical treatment facilities are so long that families frequently seek care from private providers. Further, a senior military official at another domestic installation told us that the local military treatment facility does not have a permanent developmental psychologist and as a result, some families have to wait almost 2 months for appointments. In addition, participants in five focus groups told us it has been difficult for them to obtain a particular type of autism therapy for their children, especially overseas. For example, one focus group participant in Germany told us there is a long waiting list to receive Applied Behavioral Analysis (ABA) therapy in Germany.[19] While the military does not provide ABA therapy in military treatment facilities, according to DOD officials, many families have become accustomed to receiving this service in the United States. Some DODEA area and school officials we spoke with acknowledged a shortage of autism specialists overseas.

Moreover, officials from many DOD schools we visited said it is difficult to fill and retain key positions, including special education teachers, paraprofessionals, and specialists. When a school needs additional staff to fill vacant teacher or specialist positions, candidates are first recruited from the local area. If they cannot be recruited locally, candidates are hired from the United States through a process that can take several months. Hiring delays may create staffing challenges for schools, and they may need to rely on substitutes or reallocate existing staff. For example, officials from one overseas school said that they began the school year with long-term substitutes in special education classrooms because teachers were not yet in place. In addition, officials from the same school stated that although the school began the process of filling a projected speech and language therapist vacancy in April 2011, the position was not filled until late September of that year, several weeks after the school year had begun. As a result, school officials stated they had to divide the workload among existing staff and some students received fewer services in the meantime. Officials from two additional schools noted their speech and language therapists' caseloads exceeded the DODEA standard of 30 to 50 students. Officials from one of these schools said it is unclear when they will receive another speech and

---

[19]Applied Behavioral Analysis therapy involves the use of certain principles and techniques to bring about changes in behavior.

language therapist to reduce their large caseloads. DODEA area officials also noted the difficulties in hiring speech and language therapists and other special education staff. Overall, parents in seven focus groups stated that they believed their children did not always receive all the speech and language therapy they needed, and some of these parents felt that there were shortages of these therapists. Likewise, DODEA district officials in Europe and a few school officials we spoke with overseas also acknowledged that hiring and retaining special education paraprofessionals can be difficult, citing low pay and the fact that the hiring pool—typically spouses from the local community—is a small and highly mobile population.

Families Lack Information about Obtaining Services

The family support components of each of the military branches' EFM programs are responsible for supporting military families with special needs by providing information and referral and nonclinical case management services. For example, EFM case managers at military installations may identify families' needs, provide relevant information and referrals, assist families in accessing resources, and coordinate among various resources and services. EFM family support services are available to all military families with special needs, including those with children with special educational needs. However, the support military branches offer through their EFM programs vary. For example, an EFM program official at an Army installation in Germany told us that every incoming family is provided informational materials, including those on special education, and a meeting with a case manager is scheduled to discuss the family's needs. In contrast, an EFM program official at a Navy installation in Italy said that families are expected to reach out to EFM family support staff to obtain information when they arrive.

School Liaison Officers and DODEA may also provide some information to families. School Liaison Officers generally support military leadership in coordinating with and advising parents of school-aged children on all educational issues. According to a senior DODEA official, DODEA also provides families information on special education services and processes, including documents on parental rights and responsibilities and a special education handbook.

Despite the existing support available and their general satisfaction with services once receiving them, families in 16 of our 22 focus groups said they felt the information they received about obtaining services was insufficient for their needs. Participants in four focus groups noted they faced challenges navigating DOD's complex system in order to obtain special education and medical services. Seventy of the 92 active duty servicemembers and spouses who attended our focus groups reported having one or more children enrolled in their respective branch's EFM program. While families in three of our focus groups reported they were satisfied with their respective branches' EFM programs, parents in 21of the 22 focus groups told us that the program played little to no role in helping them learn about or access special education and medical services. Further, while each of the military branches' EFM programs have case managers to assist military families in learning about and obtaining special education and medical services for their children, families in seven of our focus groups told us they lacked a central point of contact to assist them in doing so. As a result, a participant in one focus group reported feeling "lost" when trying to learn about and access such services, while another noted feeling "frustrated." Families in three of our focus groups indicated they had to be proactive and obtain information on their own, while participants in three focus groups also stated they primarily received information from other families with children with disabilities. In addition, participants in three focus groups were not aware that the EFM program provided support in learning about or accessing services. Focus group participants at one installation overseas said they did not receive any information from EFM programs regarding what types of special education services and specialists were available on base before they relocated. Officials at two schools we visited, as well as military officials at one installation, confirmed that families sometimes face challenges obtaining information and navigating the system for accessing special education and medical services.

At the DOD headquarters level, OSN has taken some steps to provide better information to families and identify their concerns, including developing outreach and marketing materials and updating website information on EFM programs for families. For example, OSN has provided resources to help strengthen education and awareness in the Army EFM program community. Further, OSN, in collaboration with the military branches, is in the process of developing online learning modules, including an overview of the EFM program. OSN has also developed a reference guide for EFM program case managers to help them access and network with community support systems. However, the extent to which these efforts are helping families obtain information and access services for their children remains unclear.

DOD Is Taking Steps to Improve EFM Programs, but Limited Oversight Hinders Its Ability to Assess and Ensure Program Effectiveness

DOD Has Taken Recent Steps to Improve Screening Processes

OSN and the military branches are taking actions to improve assignment coordination processes for military families with special needs. These efforts include, but are not limited to, families with children with disabilities who require special education services. DOD provided $5 million in fiscal year 2010 and $10 million in fiscal year 2011 to the military branches, based on their needs, to hire and train an additional 120 EFM program family support personnel to assist military families with identifying and accessing programs and services. The military branches also hired staff or identified a point of contact at all installations to support military families with special needs and trained all EFM program family support staff. As of fiscal year 2012, the branches allocated funding to maintain these additional staff.

Since its establishment in late 2010, OSN has begun several initiatives to improve EFM programs, including revising DOD policy to establish minimum requirements for the three components of the program. OSN is revising the policy in response to the 2010 NDAA in order to reflect requirements included in the legislation. Under the new policy, currently in draft, each military branch will be expected to revise and implement branch-specific guidance. According to a senior OSN official, the draft policy will include reporting requirements for the branches, such as the number of EFM families identified and screened and the number of assignment concerns. OSN officials indicated the draft policy revisions are currently undergoing internal review and could take a year or more to be finalized. OSN is also working with the Council on Accreditation to develop performance goals for the family support component of the EFM programs.[20] According to agency officials, this effort is based on the requirements set forth in the 2010 NDAA. These performance goals are intended to address the resource and referral aspects of family support services, among other things.

OSN is also undertaking another initiative, working with a contractor to conduct an analysis of each branch's current EFM program databases and case management systems. According to officials, this analysis is a first step in a long-term project to determine the feasibility of developing a joint database that would network all three components of the EFM program. If a joint database is developed, OSN officials noted that a range of relevant program officials—including DODEA staff, medical providers, and EFM case managers—would have access to components of the joint database to obtain information necessary to assist families with special needs. As of May 2012, the first phase of the analysis is complete and provides information on all the information sources and databases for each of the military branches' EFM programs, according to a senior OSN official. As a next step, OSN expects to develop common definitions and explore ways to merge or network existing databases, which officials anticipate will be completed by October 2013. However, an OSN official stated that developing a joint database will require significant buy-in from each military branch. As such, this process is anticipated to take several years, according to officials.

Office of Special Needs' Oversight of Screening Processes and Family Support Programs Is Limited

Although OSN was established to enhance and monitor the military branches' support for military families with special needs, it lacks a strong oversight role and enforcement authority. Because the military branches are responsible for implementing and enforcing EFM program requirements, OSN currently has limited authority to enforce these requirements if a military branch does not follow or effectively implement them. According to DOD policy, each military branch is required to maintain records and report annually to the Deputy Under Secretary of Defense for Military Community and Family Policy on the current number

---

[20]The Council on Accreditation is an international, independent, not-for-profit, child- and family-service and behavioral healthcare accrediting organization. It was founded in 1977 by the Child Welfare League of America and Family Service America (now the Alliance for Children and Families). Originally known as an accrediting body for family and children's agencies, the Council on Accreditation currently accredits over 45 different service areas. Among the service areas are substance abuse treatment, adult day care, services for the homeless, foster care, and inter-country adoption.

of family members identified with special needs and the effectiveness of its processes for implementing EFM program guidance.[21] However, officials from at least one branch's EFM program acknowledged they had not provided the required reports, and OSN is limited in the extent to which it can compel them to do so. DOD officials noted that while OSN does not have direct enforcement authority over the branches' EFM programs, high-level responsibility for ensuring compliance with program requirements rests with the Under Secretary of Defense for Personnel and Readiness. For example OSN, through the Under Secretary of Defense of Personnel and Readiness, may submit a report to DODEA or the secretaries of the military branches citing noncompliance. However, only the branches have the ability to take corrective action based on such letters. Further, some DOD officials expressed concern about the lack of military leadership's sustained attention and commitment to EFM programs.

DOD also currently lacks comprehensive agencywide benchmarks and performance goals with which to measure the effectiveness of the branches' EFM programs. As noted previously, OSN is in the process of developing performance goals for the family support function of the EFM program in response to requirements set forth in the 2010 NDAA. However, OSN does not currently have benchmarks and performance goals for the two other components of the program—identification/enrollment and assignment coordination. Our prior work has noted that establishing performance goals and measuring progress is a key element of effective oversight.[22] At least one military branch has included performance goals and standards in its EFM program policy. Specifically, the Air Force's EFM program instruction includes targets and benchmarks for relocations due to assignment concerns. For example, according to these benchmarks, less than 0.5 percent of families who relocate each calendar year should be relocated again as the result of unavailable educational or medical services at the initial location. Another Air Force target stipulates that 5 percent or less of EFM program reassignments in each calendar year will be due to screening failures.

---

[21]DOD Instruction 1315.19(5.4.15) and DOD Instruction 1315.19(E5.1.3).

[22]See, for example GAO, *Preventing Sexual Harassment: DOD Needs Greater Leadership Commitment and an Oversight Framework*, GAO-11-809 (Washington, D.C.: Sept. 21, 2011) and *Military Personnel: DOD's and the Coast Guard's Sexual Assault Prevention and Response Programs Face Implementation and Oversight Challenges*, GAO-08-924 (Washington, D.C.: Aug. 29, 2008).

Because DOD currently lacks performance goals and benchmarks, it cannot assess the effectiveness of the branches' EFM programs and ensure that improvements are made when needed. Without overall performance information to proactively identify emerging problem areas, some of the branches have only been able to react to specific problems after they have arisen. For example, entities within the Air Force and Navy have conducted internal audits or investigations in response to concerns regarding special education services and EFM programs. In December 2009, the Inspector General of the Air Force initiated an investigation of the Air Force's EFM program in response to complaints from a number of Air Force families with special needs.[23] The investigation substantiated many of the complaints from families, including allegations that installations did not follow required assignment coordination procedures. As of June 2012, the Air Force has not determined its plans to respond to the investigation findings. Similarly, in April 2009, the Naval Audit Service initiated an audit of the Marine Corps' EFM program.[24] While this audit focused on children's access to special education services in public schools in the United States, the Naval Audit Service identified areas for improvement in the Marine Corps' oversight and provision of EFM program services. The Marine Corps concurred with the audit's recommendations. As of June 2012, Marine Corps officials stated that most of the audit's recommendations have been addressed. They added that the remaining open recommendations are related to ongoing efforts currently being implemented, such as those intended to improve case manager training processes. Finally, in April 2010, the Naval Audit Service initiated an audit of the Navy's EDIS program to verify that the program effectively provides special education services to school-aged children overseas.[25] The audit focused on services for school-aged children enrolled in the Navy's EDIS program in the Mediterranean area. It found that there was inadequate centralized oversight over local programs as well as inadequate educational screening for families being assigned to overseas locations. The Navy Bureau of Medicine and Surgery concurred with the audit's

---

[23]Inspector General of the Air Force: Report of Investigation (ROI) - Category 1, December 2, 2009 – January 12, 2010.

[24]Naval Audit Service: Marine Corps Exceptional Family Member Program, January 14, 2011.

[25]Naval Audit Service: Department of the Navy Educational and Developmental Intervention Services, March 29, 2012.

recommendations and agreed to take actions to address them with a target completion date of October 2012.

Conclusions

In 2011, the Administration made the care and support of military families a top national security policy priority. In the 2011 White House report, the heads of 16 executive branch agencies, including the Secretary of Defense, committed to making the well-being of military families one of their highest priorities and to improve their access to services and support. Further, the Administration emphasized the importance of ensuring that military children are provided a quality education. Due to their frequent relocations, accessing educational services may be particularly difficult for military families—especially for those with children with special educational needs. DODEA and the military branches provide special education services to eligible families thorough a complex system that varies by location. While families in our focus groups were generally satisfied once their children received special education services, they faced challenges obtaining these services, in part due to the limited availability of medical and related service providers at overseas installations. In addition, families may lack sufficient information about accessing special education and related medical services. The challenges families and schools face in obtaining and providing special education services are not unique to DOD schools. However, the complexity of DOD's system for providing services—especially overseas—along with the high mobility of military families is unique. Consequently, effective overseas assignment and family support processes are essential for meeting the needs of families with children with special needs. Impediments to effective assignment coordination, such as ineffective screening processes, can result in families being assigned to overseas installations that are unable to readily meet their children's educational and medical needs. As such, it is important that the branches' screening and assignment processes for children with special needs are consistently conducted in a thorough manner.

OSN has recently taken some steps to enhance the military branches' EFM programs. However, it is unclear when some of these efforts will be completed or if they will be effectively implemented. While OSN was established in part to monitor the military branches' support for families with special needs, it has limited enforcement authority over the branches' EFM programs. Specifically, it is limited in the extent to which it can compel the branches to comply with DOD or service-level program requirements, and it has no direct means by which to hold them accountable if they fail to do so. As such, it is important that OSN develop processes to strengthen its oversight of the branches' EFM programs to ensure that they are operating effectively.

Moreover, DOD currently lacks uniform performance goals and benchmarks for all aspects of the EFM program. Because OSN is charged with monitoring EFM programs and is developing benchmarks and performance goals for the family support component of the program, it is well positioned to develop them for the other two components of the program—identification/enrollment and assignment coordination. Such an effort would give DOD the information it needs to determine whether the branches are complying with program policies and requirements. Without clear benchmarks and performance goals, DOD is limited in the extent to which it can determine the effectiveness of the branches' EFM programs and improve these programs for families with special needs. As a result, families may continue to be assigned to installations that cannot readily meet their children's special educational and medical needs.

Recommendations for Executive Action

Based on our review, we are making three recommendations.

To ensure that military families are assigned to overseas installations that can readily meet their children's special educational and medical needs, we recommend that the Secretary of Defense direct the secretaries of each branch to ensure that all military dependent children of school age are medically and educationally screened in accordance with each branch's policies and that all required educational screening forms are forwarded to DODEA for educational assignment recommendations prior to families' relocations.

To improve oversight of the military branches' programs for families with special needs, we recommend that the Secretary of Defense direct OSN to establish uniform benchmarks and performance goals for the identification/enrollment and assignment coordination components of the military branches' EFM programs. These goals can be used to determine whether EFM programs are achieving desired outcomes across DOD and identify areas for improvement. For example, such performance goals could include specific targets and benchmarks for reducing screening failures over time and reassigning families who have been sent to locations that are unable to meet their children's educational or medical needs.

To strengthen OSN's oversight over the military branches' EFM programs, we recommend that the Secretary of Defense direct OSN to develop and implement a process to assess the branches' compliance with DOD-level EFM program policies and requirements, and to identify and report any issues related to noncompliance to senior leadership for corrective action. For example, OSN could consider conducting periodic, unannounced site visits to select military installations on a periodic basis to monitor implementation of their EFM programs.

Agency Comments and Our Evaluation

We provided a draft of this report to the Department of Defense (DOD) for review and comment. DOD's comments are reproduced in appendix III. DOD also provided technical comments that we incorporated in the report as appropriate.

DOD concurred with our recommendation that all school-age military dependent children be medically and educationally screened and that all screening forms be forwarded to DODEA for placement recommendations before families relocate. DOD noted that it has a policy that requires the military branches to identify and refer school-age children with special educational needs to the appropriate DODEA reviewer for educational placement recommendations.

DOD partially concurred with our recommendation to direct OSN to establish uniform benchmarks and performance goals for two elements of the branches' EFM programs—the identification/enrollment and assignment coordination components. In its comments, DOD said it has completed the first year of an analysis of the branches' EFM programs that will provide uniform benchmarks and performance goals for these components of the program. In a subsequent discussion with DOD to clarify their written comments, a senior official confirmed that these benchmarks and performance goals are currently not in place and are still in the process of being developed. While there is no specific deadline for their completion, DOD anticipates that they will be finalized in mid-2013. Since the primary intent of this effort is to develop a joint database that will network all three components of the EFM program, it is unclear whether any benchmarks and goals resulting from the analysis will include all the elements necessary for effective oversight of the programs.

DOD partially concurred with our recommendation to provide OSN with the authority to require the branches to comply with DOD and branch-level EFM program policies and requirements. DOD said its current policies assign responsibility for ensuring compliance to senior leadership within the Office of the Secretary of Defense. In addition, DOD said the responsibility for ensuring the branches' compliance with its forthcoming revised policy on EFM program compliance will be assigned to the Assistant Secretary of Defense for Readiness and Force Management to whom OSN will report any issues regarding noncompliance. When this occurs, DOD said the Assistant Secretary will direct the branches to take corrective action. We revised our report to clarify that high-level responsibility for ensuring the branches' compliance with EFM program requirements rests with the Under Secretary of Defense for Personnel and Readiness. We also modified our recommendation to direct DOD to require OSN to develop and implement a process to assess the branches' compliance with EFM program policies and requirements and to report any issues related to noncompliance to senior leadership for corrective action. We believe this would allow OSN to better evaluate the extent to which the branches are complying with the revised policy.

In overall comments on our report, DOD said that despite some families' comments in our focus groups that their children lacked services such as speech and language therapy, its monitoring reports over the past 10 years have indicated no lack of services due to an inadequate number of special education teachers or specialists. In our report, we noted that families' comments about challenges obtaining special education services were generally corroborated by DODEA administrative offices and individual schools overseas. For example, officials from DOD schools we visited told us they have difficulties filling and retaining key positions, such as special education teachers, paraprofessionals, and specialists. In addition, some officials said that caseloads for certain special education service providers can exceed accepted standards.

In addition, DOD said the perspectives obtained from families during our focus groups are presented as facts in our report, and noted that caution must be exercised when drawing conclusions about the accessibility of services based on a sample of individual opinions. In our report, we acknowledged that our focus groups cannot be generalized to all parents of children with special needs, nor are they representative of the entire population of parents. Because common responses and recurring themes across focus groups provide some degree of validation that experiences are not limited to specific individuals, we identified throughout the report the number of focus groups where particular perspectives were discussed. In addition, we did not rely entirely on focus groups for evidence in the report, but rather used several different methods to support our conclusions. For example, we interviewed officials from DODEA administrative offices, military branches, and individual schools who corroborated many themes that emerged during our focus groups.

We are sending copies of this report to the appropriate congressional committees, the Secretary of Defense, and other interested parties. The report also is available at no charge on the GAO website at http://www.gao.gov.

If you or your staff members have any questions about this report, please contact me at (202) 512-7215 or scottg@gao.gov. Contact points for our Offices of Congressional Relations and Public Affairs may be found on the last page of this report. GAO staff who made major contributions to this report are listed in appendix IV.

George A. Scott
Director, Education, Workforce,
    and Income Security Issues

Appendix I: Scope and Methodology

The objectives of this report were to determine (1) how the Department of Defense (DOD) provides special education services, and any associated challenges for families and schools; (2) how DOD entities coordinate to assign families to overseas locations, and how schools might be affected; (3) what challenges, if any, families face in obtaining DOD services for their children with special educational needs and accessing related information; and (4) what steps, if any, DOD is taking to enhance screening and overseas assignment for families with children with special educational needs.

Site Visits to Selected Military Installations and DOD Schools

In order to obtain information on how DOD schools provide special education services, and to identify challenges families face in obtaining these services and schools face in providing them, we conducted site visits to five military installations in Europe and in two states. During these site visits, we visited nine schools on four military installations in Germany, and two schools on a military installation in Italy. Domestically, we also visited three schools on an installation in North Carolina and two schools on an installation in South Carolina. We also held telephone interviews with school and other officials from a military installation in Japan. (See table 1 for more information on the installations and schools we visited.) During our school visits we conducted 22 focus groups with parents of children with special education needs enrolled in these schools. We also interviewed school officials, including principals, teachers, and specialists, at 15 of the 17 schools included in our study to learn about the challenges schools face in providing special education services, and the strategies they employ to respond to those challenges. We also toured schools and obtained documents. In addition, we interviewed Department of Defense Education Activity (DODEA) area and district officials, and officials from the Exceptional Family Member (EFM) program and the Educational and Developmental Intervention Services (EDIS) programs on each of the installations we visited. Site visit locations were selected to obtain ranges in the number of students with special education needs enrolled in DOD schools in particular districts and the severity of needs the schools overseas were equipped to serve. We also strove to achieve variation in urban and remote areas, as well as the four armed service branches. In addition, we considered recommendations from DODEA and subject matter experts in our selection of site visit locations.

Table 1: Site Visit Installation and School Selection

Selected district	Selected military installation	Number and type of school
South Carolina/Fort Stewart/Cuba	Marine Corps/Navy Tri-Command (South Carolina)	1 Elementary School 1 Elementary/Middle School
North Carolina	Fort Bragg (Army) (North Carolina)	2 Elementary Schools 1 Intermediate School
Mediterranean	Naval Support Activity Naples (Italy)	1 Elementary School 1 Middle/High School
Kaiserslautern	Ramstein Air Base (Germany)	1 Elementary School 1 Intermediate School
	Spangdahlem Air Base/Eifel community (Germany)	2 Elementary Schools
	U.S. Army Garrison Kaiserslautern (Germany)	1 Elementary School 1 Elementary/Middle School 1 Middle School 1 High School
	U.S. Army Garrison Baumholder (Germany)	1 Elementary School
Japan (by video teleconference)	Commander Fleet Activities Yokosuka (Naval Base, Japan)	1 Elementary School

Source: GAO.

Focus Groups with Parents of Children with Special Education Needs Enrolled in DOD Schools

We conducted 22 focus groups at all of the schools included in our study, including 17 at overseas locations and five at domestic locations, covering over 100 service members, their spouses, and DOD civilians across all four branches of the military, in order to obtain the views of parents regarding the challenges they face in learning about and obtaining special education services for their children with special needs. One of our overseas focus groups was conducted via video teleconference, rather than in person, to mitigate travel costs. We are confident that using this method did not substantially impact our findings. For each location, all parents of children with an individualized education program (IEP) were invited to participate. A list of sites we spoke with can be found in table 1.

A focus group protocol was developed to help the moderator gather information from these parents about their experiences with special education services at DODEA schools. The protocol contained questions about the types of services their children received, degree of satisfaction with those services, experiences with the Exceptional Family Member (EFM) program and with the screening process for obtaining special education services, and a comparison to services provided at other locations. In addition, it included questions on any complaints that may have been communicated to DODEA, and the resolution of those complaints. Notes were taken by at least one, but usually multiple, GAO note-takers. These notes were integrated into transcripts of the focus groups, which were then organized by question. For each question, a GAO analyst reviewed notes from all the focus groups to identify themes across the different groups, in order to provide insights into the range of concerns and support for these topics. While the results of these focus groups cannot be generalized to all parents of children with special needs, nor are they representative of the population of parents, common responses across groups and recurring themes provide some degree of validation. Because of these limitations, our study was supported by several methodologies, of which the focus groups were one part, to support our conclusions.

Interviews with Agency Officials and Other Organizations

To address all of the report's objectives, we interviewed relevant officials from DODEA, the Office of Special Needs, and the military services' EFM program headquarters offices. We also met with individual subject matter experts and representatives from the National Council on Disability and the Specialized Training of Military Parents, an organization focused on providing support and advice to military families with special needs. In addition, we reviewed relevant federal laws and regulations. We also reviewed agency documents and program guidance, such as DODEA's directory of special education services in overseas communities, DODEA's special education procedural guide, service-level EFM program instructions, and DOD instructions for the provision of special education and related services. We also reviewed prior GAO reports on military dependents and elementary and secondary education.

Data Collection and Analysis

To obtain information about the number and characteristics of children with special needs who attend DOD schools, we reviewed data from DODEA's Excent and Aspen databases, including enrollment by disability type, location, and military branch or other governmental affiliation, as of January 2012. As part of our data request, we asked questions about the reliability of the data, such as whether there are audits of the data or routine quality control procedures in place. We found limitations with the enrollment data resulting from the transition between systems, but determined that the data provided by DOD were sufficiently reliable to accurately provide an approximation of enrollment figures as of January 2012. We also examined data from DODEA's Screening and Assignment Concerns database to determine the number of screenings and assignment concerns reported between 2005 and 2012, as well as the nature of the assignment concerns from the most recent school year. We tested the screening and assignment concerns database for errors and found the data to be sufficiently reliable for the purposes of reporting the number of screenings and the number and nature of assignment concerns.

Appendix II: DODEA Categories and Definitions of Disabilities

1. Physical Impairments	Students whose educational performance is adversely affected by a physical impairment that requires environmental and/or academic modifications including, but not limited to, the following: visually impaired, hearing impaired, orthopedically impaired, and other health impaired.
Autism Spectrum Disorder	This term includes Pervasive Developmental Disorder, Asperger's syndrome, as well as the diagnosis of autism. It is a developmental disability significantly affecting verbal and nonverbal communication and social interaction, generally evident before age 3 that adversely affects educational performance. The term does not include students with characteristics of the disability "serious emotional disturbance."
Deaf	A hearing loss or deficit so severe that the student is impaired in processing linguistic information through hearing, with or without amplification, to the extent that his or her educational performance is adversely affected.
Deaf-Blindness	Concomitant hearing and visual impairments. This disability causes such severe communication, developmental, and educational problems that they cannot be accommodated in special education programs solely for students with deafness or students with blindness.
Hearing Impairment	An impairment in hearing, whether permanent or fluctuating that adversely affects a student's educational performance, but is not included under the definition of deafness.
Other Health Impairment (OHI)	Though not exhaustive, OHI may include limited strength, vitality, or alertness due to chronic or acute health problems that adversely affect a student's educational performance, including but not limited to heart condition, tuberculosis, rheumatic fever, nephritis, asthma, sickle cell anemia, hemophilia, epilepsy, lead poisoning, leukemia, diabetes or attention deficit disorder with or without hyperactivity.
Orthopedic Impairment	A severe physical impairment that adversely affects a student's educational performance. The term includes congenital impairments, impairments caused by disease (e.g., poliomyelitis, bone tuberculosis, etc.), and impairments from other causes such as cerebral palsy, amputations, and fractures or burns causing contractures.
Traumatic Brain Injury	An acquired injury to the brain caused by an external physical force, resulting in total or partial functional disability or psychosocial impairment, or both, that adversely affects a student's educational performance. The term applies to open or closed head injuries resulting in impairments in

one or more areas, such as cognition, language, memory, attention, reasoning, abstract thinking, judgment, or problem-solving; sensory, perceptual, and motor abilities; psychosocial behavior; physical functions; information processing, and speech. The term does not apply to brain injuries that are congenital or degenerative, or brain injuries induced by birth trauma.

Visual Impairment, including Blindness	Impairment in vision that, even with correction, adversely affects a student's educational performance. The term includes both partial sight and blindness.

2. Emotional Impairments

A condition that has been confirmed by clinical evaluation and diagnosis and that, over a long period of time and to a marked degree, adversely affects educational performance and that exhibits one or more of the following characteristics:

1. An inability to learn that cannot be explained by intellectual, sensory, or health factors.

1. An inability to build or maintain satisfactory interpersonal relationships with peers and teachers.

2. Inappropriate types of behavior under normal circumstances.

3. A tendency to develop physical symptoms or fears associated with personal or school problems.

4. A general pervasive mood of unhappiness or depression.

This includes students who are schizophrenic, but does not include students who are socially maladjusted, unless it is determined that they are seriously emotionally disturbed. The term emotional impairment does not usually include (a) antisocial behavior, (b) parent-child problems, (c) conduct disorders, (d) interpersonal problems, or (e) other problems that are not the result of a severe mental disorder.

3. Communication Impairments

Communication Impairment includes two disabilities: speech disorders and language disorders. Students whose educational performance is adversely affected by a developmental or acquired communication disorder to include voice, fluency, articulation, receptive, and/or expressive language.

Language/Phonological
Disorders

Language/phonological disorders are characterized by an
impairment/delay in receptive and/or expressive language including
semantics, orphology/syntax, phonology and/or pragmatics. This
impairment does not include students whose language problems are due
to English as a second language or dialect difference.

Speech Disorders

1. *Articulation disorder* is characterized by substitutions, distortions,
   and/or omissions of phonemes that are not commensurate with
   expected developmental age norms, that are not the result of limited
   English proficiency or dialect difference, and that may cause
   unintelligible conversational speech.

2. *Fluency disorder* is characterized by atypical rate, rhythm, repetitions,
   and/or secondary behavior(s) that interferes with communication or is
   inconsistent with age/development.

3. *Voice disorder* is characterized by abnormal pitch, intensity,
   resonance, duration, and/or quality that is inappropriate for
   chronological age or gender.

4. Learning Impairments

Learning Impairment includes two disabilities: specific learning disability
and intellectual disability.

Specific Learning Disability

Specific learning disability is a disorder in one or more of the basic
psychological processes involved in understanding or in using spoken or
written language that may manifest itself as an imperfect ability to listen,
think, speak, read, write, spell, remember, or do mathematical
calculations. The term includes such conditions as perceptual disabilities,
brain injury, minimal brain dysfunction, dyslexia, and developmental
aphasia. The term does not include learning problems that are primarily
the result of visual, hearing, or motor disabilities; of mental retardation or
emotional disturbance; or of environmental, cultural, or economic
disadvantage.

Intellectual Disability

Intellectual disability is significantly sub-average intellectual functioning
existing concurrently with deficits in adaptive behavior and manifested
during the developmental period that adversely affects a student's
educational performance. Significant sub-average general intellectual
functioning is documented by a comprehensive intelligence test score that
is two or more standard deviations below the mean.

5. Developmental Delay

The term developmental delay refers to a significant discrepancy in the actual functioning of an infant, toddler, or child birth through age 7, when compared with the functioning of a nondisabled infant, toddler, or child of the same chronological age in the following areas: physical, cognitive, communication, social or emotional, and adaptive development as measured using standardized evaluation instruments and confirmed by clinical observation and judgment. A child classified with a developmental delay before age 7 may maintain that eligibility classification through age 10. Developmental delay does not refer to a condition in which a child is slightly or momentarily lagging in development. The presence of a developmental delay is an indication that the developmental processes are significantly affected and that, without special intervention, it is likely that the educational performance will be affected when the child reaches school age.

There are five developmental areas of concern in the definition of developmental delay:

1. *Physical Development* - Fine/gross motor skills used for coordinated use of muscles and body control in actions such as balance, standing, walking, climbing, object manipulation, cutting, and pre-writing activities.

2. *Communication Development* - Ability to understand and use language and the phonological processes.

3. *Cognitive Development* - Ability to receive information, process relationships, and apply knowledge.

4. *Social/Emotional Development* - Ability to develop and maintain functional interpersonal relationships and to exhibit social and emotional behaviors appropriate to the setting.

5. *Adaptive/Self-Help Development* - Ability to deal with environmental expectations and use functional daily living skills.

Appendix III: Comments from the Department of Defense

OFFICE OF THE ASSISTANT SECRETARY OF DEFENSE
4000 DEFENSE PENTAGON
WASHINGTON, D.C. 20301-4000

READINESS AND FORCE
MANAGEMENT

AUG   3 2012

Mr. George A. Scott
Director, Education, Workforce, and Income Security Issues
United States Government Accountability Office
441 G Street, NW
Washington, DC 20548

Dear Mr. Scott:

Thank you for the opportunity to review and provide comments on the report, *MILITARY DEPENDENT STUDENTS: Better Oversight Needed to Improve Services for Children with Special Needs*. We consider care for children with special needs to be of the utmost importance for military families with direct impact on the effectiveness and readiness of the force.

The report tackles the challenging task of sorting through different but related systems (special education in the Department of Defense (DoD) schools, the Exceptional Family Member Program and overseas screening), administered by different organizations, that fall under different chains of command. We agree with the sentiment addressed in the three recommendations that the Exceptional Family Member Program is important and that the policy must be enforced, but we wish to provide additional clarification on the recommendations (attached) and content of the report.

With regard to availability of special education at DoD schools, the DoD school systems, not unlike public school systems in the United States, staff schools with special education providers dependent upon the size and location of the schools. Small isolated schools will serve students with special educational needs if they arrive; however, for assignment purposes, the DoD Education Activity (DoDEA) reviewer will not recommend those locations for families with children who require special education. The review process is intended to match families to the locations that have the appropriate services in place to maximize resources.

Family members reported that they believed their children lacked services such as speech and language therapy. Our review of the DoD school vacancies indicated that there had been no long-term vacancies other than the hiring lag that can occur when running an overseas school system. In instances when a teacher or specialist leaves during the school year, it can take two to four months to hire and re-locate a replacement to an overseas location. During this interim period, DoDEA reallocates specialists to cover the caseload at the gapped location. DoD monitoring reports for the past ten years have indicated no lack of services for children due to an inadequate number of teachers or specialists.

The report is based on input from fewer than 100 families and providers, and in some cases individual opinions are presented as facts. Caution must be exercised when drawing conclusions about accessibility of services based on the small sample and individual opinions.

An example from the report is the perception that military families have less access to developmental pediatricians than civilian counterparts. The military employs 6% of all developmental pediatricians in the United States. Given that the military represents only 1% of the population, military families have six times the access to developmental pediatricians as their civilian counterparts. The random probability sample of fewer than 100 families relative to the total number of families accessing special education in the DoD schools indicates the need for caution in drawing conclusions about accessibility of services. It is important for policy makers to understand the limitations of the data set when making decisions about the availability of services.

Please contact the Primary Action Officer if you have additional questions or require any clarification.

Sincerely,

Charles E. Milam
Principal Director
(Military Community and Family Policy)

Enclosure:
As stated

2

GAO DRAFT REPORT DATED JUNE 27, 2012
GAO-12-680 (GAO CODE 131101)

"MILITARY DEPENDENT STUDENTS: BETTER OVERSIGHT NEEDED TO
IMPROVE SERVICES FOR CHILDREN WITH SPECIAL NEEDS"

DEPARTMENT OF DEFENSE COMMENTS
TO THE GAO RECOMMENDATIONS

RECOMMENDATION 1: The GAO recommends that the Secretary of Defense direct the secretaries of each branch to ensure that all military dependent children of school age are medically and educationally screened in accordance with each branch's policies and that all required educational screening forms are forwarded to DoD Education Activity (DoDEA) for educational placement recommendations prior to families' relocations.

DoD RESPONSE: Concur. DoD Instruction 1315.19 requires the Military Services to identify children of school age who have special educational needs to the appropriate DoDEA reviewer for educational placement recommendations.

RECOMMENDATION 2: The GAO recommends that the Secretary of Defense direct the Undersecretary for Personnel and Readiness to direct Office of Community Support for Military Families with Special Needs (OSN) to establish uniform benchmarks and performance goals for the identification/enrollment and assignment coordination components of the military branches Exceptional Family Member (EFM) programs.

DoD RESPONSE: Partially Concur. The OSN has completed the first year of an analysis of the Exceptional Family Member Program (EFMP) that will provide uniform benchmarks and performance goals for the enrollment and assignment coordination components of the program. A separate effort has developed accreditation standards for the EFMP family support component, which are being piloted currently by the Council on Accreditation. This effort will result in uniform benchmarks and performance goals for EFMP family support programs.

RECOMMENDATION 3: The GAO recommends that the Secretary of Defense provide OSN with the authority to require that the branches comply with DoD and service level EFM program policies and requirements.

DoD RESPONSE: Partially Concur. DoD policies assign the responsibility for ensuring compliance to senior leadership within the Office of the Secretary of Defense. In the case of the policy being developed for the EFMP that responsibility will be assigned to the Assistant Secretary of Defense for Readiness and Force Management (ASD(R&FM)). The OSN will report to the ASD(R&FM) any issues with non-compliance. The ASD(R&FM) will direct the Services to take corrective action.

Appendix IV: GAO Contact and Staff Acknowledgments

GAO Contact	George Scott, 202-512-7215 or scottg@gao.gov
Staff Acknowledgments	In addition to the contact named above, Elizabeth Sirois, Assistant Director; Divya Bali, Jennifer Cook, and Charlene J. Lindsay made significant contributions to this report. Also contributing to this report were Deborah Bland, Kate van Gelder, Mimi Nguyen, Steven Putansu, James Rebbe, Michael Silver, and Rachael Valliere.

Related GAO Products

Education of Military Dependent Students: Better Information Needed to Assess Student Performance. GAO-11-231. Washington, D.C.: March 1, 2011.

DOD Schools: Additional Reporting Could Improve Accountability for Academic Achievement of Students with Dyslexia. GAO-08-70. Washington, D.C.: December 6, 2007.

Military Personnel: Medical, Family Support, and Educational Services Are Available for Exceptional Family Members. GAO-07-317R. Washington, D.C.: March 16, 2007.

DOD Schools: Limitations in DOD-Sponsored Study on Transfer Alternatives Underscore Need for Additional Assessment. GAO-05-469. Washington, D.C.: April 26, 2005.

www.ingramcontent.com/pod-product-compliance
Lightning Source LLC
Chambersburg PA
CBHW080915290526
45795CB00007BA/2527